D1716541

OFF-ROAD RACING

HOT TOPICS

BY KATE MIKOLEY

 Gareth Stevens
PUBLISHING

Please visit our website, www.garethstevens.com. For a free color catalog of all our high-quality books, call toll free 1-800-542-2595 or fax 1-877-542-2596.

Cataloging-in-Publication Data

Names: Mikoley, Kate, author.
Title: Off-road racing / Kate Mikoley.
Description: New York : Gareth Stevens Publishing, [2020] | Series: Motorsports Maniacs | Includes index.
Identifiers: LCCN 2019003291| ISBN 9781538240946 (paperback) | ISBN 9781538240960 (library bound) | ISBN 9781538240953 (6 pack)
Subjects: LCSH: Off-road racing--Juvenile literature. | All terrain vehicle racing--Juvenile literature. | Off-road vehicles--Juvenile literature.
Classification: LCC GV1037 .M55 2020 | DDC 796.72--dc23
LC record available at https://lccn.loc.gov/2019003291

First Edition

Published in 2020 by
Gareth Stevens Publishing
111 East 14th Street, Suite 349
New York, NY 10003

Copyright © 2020 Gareth Stevens Publishing

Designer: Sarah Liddell
Editor: Kate Mikoley

Photo credits: Cover, p. 1 Nachaliti/Shutterstock.com; dirt background used throughout Yibo Wang/Shutterstock.com; tire mark texture used throughout Slay/Shutterstock.com; p. 5 AFP/Stringer/AFP/Getty Images; p. 7 The Enthusiast Network/Contributor/The Enthusiast Network/Getty Images; p. 9 HeyPhoto/Shutterstock.com; p. 11 Axtem/ Shutterstock.com; p. 13 Edu Silva 2ev/Shutterstock.com; p. 15 Anadolu Agency/ Contributor/Anadolu Agency/Getty Images; p. 17 Christian Peterson/Staff/Getty Images Sport/Getty Images; p. 19 nuwatphoto/Shutterstock.com; p. 21 Mike Powell/Staff/Getty Images Sport/Getty Images; p. 23 Matt Sullivan/Stringer/Getty Images Sport/Getty Images; p. 25 Pascal Rondeau/Staff/Getty Images SPort/Getty images; p. 27 FRANCK FIFE/ Contributor/AFP/Getty Images; p. 29 AFP Contributor/Contributor/AFP/Getty Images.

Printed in the United States of America

CPSIA compliance information: Batch #CS19GS: For further information contact Gareth Stevens, New York, New York at 1-800-542-2595.

CONTENTS

A ROUGH RIDE

In some motorsports, racing is all about which car speeds around a track the fastest. But in off-road racing, the races don't take place on a smooth track. These races happen on **terrain** that is often bumpy, muddy, and covered in dirt!

TEST DRIVE

OFF-ROAD RACES ARE
OFTEN HELD IN DESERTS.

OFF-ROAD HISTORY

After World War II, racing **motorcycles** on off-road trails became fairly common. Since then, many people have enjoyed even more kinds of off-road racing. In the 1960s, a man named Ed Pearlman started the National Off-Road Racing Association (NORRA).

TEST DRIVE

MANY MOTORSPORTS HAVE GROUPS THAT OVERSEE RACES, CALLED SANCTIONING BODIES. NORRA WAS THOUGHT TO BE THE FIRST SANCTIONING BODY DIRECTED ONLY AT OFF-ROAD RACING.

ALL KINDS OF EVENTS

There are many kinds of off-road races. Some trails don't have any markings to tell drivers where to go. In some races, the **routes** between certain points can be made up. Other races, however, have clear routes drivers must follow.

TEST DRIVE

IN MOST OFF-ROAD RACES, **VEHICLES** HAVE TO MAKE IT FROM ONE PLACE TO ANOTHER. THEY OFTEN HAVE TO HIT CERTAIN POINTS IN BETWEEN, TOO.

Many vehicles are used in off-road racing—from cars and motorcycles to trucks and all-terrain vehicles (ATVs). Vehicles are usually separated, or sorted, in races. Motorcycles only race against other motorcycles, and cars only race against other cars.

TEST DRIVE

AN ATV IS A SMALL, OPEN VEHICLE, COMMONLY WITH FOUR WHEELS. HANDLEBARS ARE USED TO **STEER**. ATVS ARE MADE TO BE ABLE TO DRIVE OFF ROADS.

DIRT BIKE RACING

A motorcycle made for racing off roads is often called a dirt bike. Dirt bikes are commonly lighter than the kinds of motorcycles that drive on roads. Dirt bikes can be seen in many kinds of off-road races.

TEST DRIVE

MOTOCROSS IS A TYPE OF RACE WHERE RIDERS ON DIRT BIKES **COMPETE**, OFTEN DOING SHOCKING JUMPS AND TRICKS.

Another kind of off-road racing where dirt bikes are used is called enduro. The name comes from the word "endurance," which means having the power to do something hard for a long time. These races are long and may have **obstacles**.

TEST DRIVE

IN AN ENDURO RACE, DRIVERS
OFTEN RIDE THROUGH WOODS
AND HAVE TO CROSS WATER.

TRUCKS OFF THE ROAD!

Another vehicle commonly used in off-road racing is a truck. A pickup truck is a small truck with an open back. Trucks used in off-road racing sometimes look a little like pickup trucks you'd see driving on the street, but they're much more powerful!

TEST DRIVE

OFF-ROAD RACING CAN BE VERY
DANGEROUS, OR UNSAFE. THERE ARE
OFTEN CRASHES AND, AT TIMES,
PEOPLE HAVE EVEN DIED.

WHAT'S A UTV?

Unlike trucks and motorcycles, many off-road racing vehicles don't look like anything you'd see on the street. UTVs are vehicles that look sort of like ATVs. However, they're bigger, can carry more than one person, and have a steering wheel instead of handlebars.

TEST DRIVE

UTV STANDS FOR UTILITY
TERRAIN VEHICLE. THE WORD "UTILITY"
MEANS SOMETHING IS USEFUL.

THE BIG RACE

One of the biggest races in off-road racing is called the Baja 1000. It takes place in the Mexican state of Baja California. In its early days, the event was called the Mexican 1000 and it was run by NORRA.

TEST DRIVE

TODAY THE BAJA 1000 IS HELD BY
A GROUP CALLED SCORE INTERNATIONAL.

The race now known as the Baja 1000 has gone on for more than 50 years. Many kinds of vehicles race in different classes in this event. Drivers come from all over the world to take part in the well-known race.

Jimmie Johnson

TEST DRIVE

OVER THE YEARS, MANY FAMOUS
PEOPLE HAVE DRIVEN IN THE BAJA 1000,
SUCH AS ACTOR PATRICK DEMPSEY AND
NASCAR DRIVER JIMMIE JOHNSON.

23

Though its name makes it sound like the race is 1,000 miles (1,609 km), the Baja 1000 has actually been many different lengths throughout the years. Some races have been around 800 miles (1,287 km). Others have been longer than 1,000 miles (1,609 km)!

TEST DRIVE

THE BAJA 1000 HAS HAD MANY
DIFFERENT ROUTES THROUGHOUT THE
YEARS, BUT IT ALWAYS TAKES
PLACE IN THE DESERT.

RACING AROUND THE WORLD

Off-road racing is loved all over the world. The Dakar Rally is a race that originally went through parts of Europe and Africa. Since 2009, it's been held in South America. When cars race, a second person rides with the driver, reading them directions.

TEST DRIVE

THE DAKAR RALLY OFTEN COVERS BIG,
SANDY HILLS. THE WEATHER CAN CHANGE
A LOT, MAKING IT A HARD RACE.

WINNING THE RACE

Sometimes winners get prize money. Other times, they may get a **trophy**. Often, groups that oversee races have a points system for a group, or series, of races. Drivers earn points for each race and the person with the most points wins the series.

TEST DRIVE

SOME OFF-ROAD RACING
TRUCKS HAVE GONE FASTER THAN
100 MILES (161 KM) PER HOUR!

OFF-ROAD RACING
SAFETY TIPS

OFF-ROAD RACERS SHOULD:

- KNOW THE RULES OF THEIR RACE AND FOLLOW THEM.

- WEAR SAFETY GEAR, SUCH AS A HEAD AND NECK GUARD AND A HELMET.

- BE AWARE OF THINGS ON THE COURSE, SUCH AS TREES, THAT COULD HURT THE DRIVER IF HIT.

- WATCH OUT FOR OTHER VEHICLES AND PEOPLE WATCHING THE RACE.

FOR MORE INFORMATION

BOOKS

Abdo, Kenny. *ATVs*. Minneapolis, MN: Abdo Zoom, 2018.

Levit, Joe. *Motorsports Trivia: What You Never Knew About Car Racing, Monster Truck Events, and More Motor Mania*. North Mankato, MN: Capstone Press, 2019.

Weber, M. *Wild Moments on Dirt Bikes*. North Mankato, MN: Capstone Press, 2018.

WEBSITES

ATV Safety
kidshealth.org/en/teens/atv-safety.html
Learn how to stay safe on an ATV.

Extreme: MotoX Motocross
ducksters.com/sports/extrememotox.php
Read more about the exciting world of motocross here.

GLOSSARY

compete: to try to win a contest with others

motorcycle: a vehicle that has two wheels and is powered by a machine called a motor

obstacle: something that blocks a path

route: a course that people travel

steer: to control the direction of something that moves, such as a car

terrain: the type of land in an area

trophy: a prize awarded to the winner of a race

vehicle: an object that moves people from one place to another, such as a car

INDEX